Up
the Hill

Ron Benson
Lynn Bryan
Kim Newlove
Liz Stenson
Iris Zammit

CONSULTANTS
Florence Brown
Estella Clayton
Susan Elliott-Johns
Charolette Player
Shari Schwartz
Lynn Swanson
Helen Tomassini
Debbie Toope

Prentice Hall Ginn

Contents

Apples

by Iris Zammit
Illustrated by Marie-Claude Favreau

I like apples.

Red ones,

Green ones,

Juicy and sweet.

Big ones,

Little ones,

My favourite treat.

I like apples.

Big Duck's Walk

by Liz Stenson
Illustrated by Sylvie Daigneault

Big Duck goes for a walk

down the hill

into the water

out of the water

up the hill

15

into the yard for dinner.